MW01602131

Geoffrey Movius | Selected Poems | 1960–2010

TRANSIT

This copy for Inge, with love,

Geoffrey Movius

July 2014

Pressed Wafer | Boston

Some of these poems have been published in the current or an earlier form in the following: *Agenda* XIII; *Bennington Review*; *Boston Review*; *Chicago Review*; *Harvard Advocate*; *Harvard Review*; *Little Balkans Review*; *Little Magazine*; *Mudfish*; *Peacefeelers*; *Ploughshares*; *Silo*; *Tufts Literary Magazine*; *Tufts Observer*; *Tufts Review*; *WIP*; and in the anthology *Messages*, ed. X. J. Kennedy, Little Brown, 1973.

ISBN 978-0-9831975-7-7

Pressed Wafer
9 Columbus Square
Boston, Massachusetts 02116
pressedwafer.com

For Barbara

Contents

A prefatory note

This collection of work has been put together from poems written over the last fifty years or so. They are in many cases addressed to, or relate to, people who have helped shape my life. I can never hope to name everyone who has mattered to me deeply over so long, but I want to sing out some to whom one or another of these poems have a strong connection. Family, friends and colleagues have given me energy they never knew about. In particular, the following are strongly present: Carlos, Charles, George, Gerrit, Gordon, Grey, Hal, Jim, Joe, John, Kate, Katherine, Ken, Lou, Lucy, Martha, Stephen, and, beyond all others, my dear wife, Barbara. Bill Corbett has been a friend since the Sixties, that hallowed time, and has seen fit to bring forth this book. I am grateful to him. The order of contents is not chronological, but is hardly random.

SEASONS

Midwinter

The crowds start to hurry, sharp gusts whittling
tears down their cheeks. It is five o'clock
on this blue-iced street, and subway uprush—electricity
and heavy human air—explodes through grates in billows
of half-thoughts, goads to those who press along, breaths
one wide cloud at eye level. Evening's teenage skinheads
dance on the bricks, dervishes of malign joy, celebrating
a world slipped from nets of centuries, hip to its chaos.

But among empty buildings, down narrow back walks
where winos scavenge, shake, hug themselves to sleep,
or here in this roiling burst of people's smells,
lust dressed willy-nilly in old boots, torn coats,
long scarves, visored hats blinking tiny lights,
it's time—even the Time shown by crystals in books,
or in horoscopes whispered by young girls alone—
to bear into our world some dream of a walled and gated city,
some glister of many-colored domes on a far hill's curve,
some retinal ghost-image of possible order, possible reason,
some great, new, rare, welcome physics of the heart.

Another freeze

Just about now it becomes harder to focus
on meaning because of the cold and flocks
of birds across dark fields toward a woods
at the edge of vision, fringes of last light.

Left to ourselves we begin to make stories
in our heads about it all becoming clear—
what this mission was about, that is—
and to whom we should expect to report.

Mindful that we may be kidding ourselves
we start to move back toward the houses
we left earlier on in this surprising trip
so that we may tonight be warm and safe.

And in the now slate air, bitter snow, wind,
after a stumble or two, birds still clouding
overhead, as they too rush for safety, we
arrive, are welcomed, find ourselves home.

January thaw

There was color in some trees at noon,
yellow on willows, red in maples,
giving false sign of risen sap,
the gospel of renewal mere heat and light,
more grim cold still to come, grey days
when it will be necessary to live
and love without color or warmth.

Southerlies since Tuesday have left
the ground soft, wet on surfaces
where icemelt floated up, spread mud
in meadows, where yesterday our feet
made no prints. Time to be wary—
vulnerable as we are in this jazzed-up
charnel house, winter's baited trap,
dangerous ice crackling and sagging,
even the dark woods fully armed.

February

Pines shuck snow at far edges
of white fields, wind relentless.
Inside his home, a man, safe tonight,
measures what he sees and is pleased.

Leap year

Why go so far against the form—
an odd door in an odd house,
a snowdrop, early, cased in ice?
What is it drives him to be walking
where there is no road? He argues
with shadows, decides the outcomes
of dreams that have no endings.

Difficulties—a fridge not making ice,
a shirt with a burn mark, a missing page,
a leftover day in this unremarkable year.
The wood won't meet itself, strayed
as it is, grain and warmth to blame,
so his door won't close. Push. Pull.

Equinox

In change all growth
and harm are carried,
a truth borne in upon his world,
as here
in what he sees.

Laid on gardens
through conspiracy
of shades and curtains,
late March snow,
crocus assassin.

Green and yellow,
daffodils extruded,
bent headless,
buried without
their dreams.

Whitethroats scrape
and chivvy
empty husks,
their suet gone.
Bluejays rant.

Anger with no substance,
no idea of the cause.
"What should I do?"
"What should I say?"
nicker unanswered.

Between two kinds of cold,
it melts then kills.
Nothing stays more perfect
than ever before
at winter's edge.

May

Come spring they start again.
The thing she said was love
was love.

Slipped April's lead
and hankering, he plods
the whole field's length,

building cages with his eyes
to hold wildcats and hawks.
Earth falls apart behind him.

On the hill, still home,
she reads and bakes.
She sings, holding

the sun up, setting out
a garden in her mind.
She thinks of every possibility.

Red pines unbrace and whistle.
Stones shift and flake.
An idea has melted in the brook.

Summers by the cove

Even from where I lounge in my chair in the studio
I can see their muscles pumped up in white undershirts—
two young guys in a black dory rowing hard
in the village fair race up and down our cove.
When they've reached the head they slow, turn,
and rest, waiting for the signal to start back.
They laugh and chat as though this were a hike
in the woods up on Dogtown, drink bottled water,
then set up again and at "Ready," oars bite deep
and they're gone from my window frame, wake
washing up in marsh grass, blue sky in waves.

More than 50 years ago, I stood on the bridge watching
Wimp Davis and his cousin row this cove race against
a couple of Novies from Halifax. Beaten badly,
they took solace in beer and rum sloshed down in sequence—
"Portagee sandwiches," Wimp said. He's been making
grass taller on the hill beside this cove for 35 years at least,
done in by failure, his father, and booze. Here comes a kayaker
all in red. I bet Wimp never saw a kayak in his short sad life.

In the country

The switchback drops. He leans
around a sapling, drifts downhill,
uncertain of time, hearing birds
tell specifically their places,
announce discoveries of food,
a palate's joy, or desire's dark,
even pulsing in this heat,
this weight of unborn breezes.

What if, written on a tree, or spelled
out in sticks by a brook, his life's goal
should suddenly be revealed, one fact
amid harangues of deerflies
and rush of blood at spine's base?
Sweat runs from his hair,
his stomach eats itself,
his boots are too big.

In bed, another day vanquished,
he saves a long-legged insect
from a spider's web. Later, he feels
movement on his arm and swats.
"Nature depends on the moment
of our knowing it," he opines, dreamward,
liberator and destroyer of light wings.

Fishing

The hardest part is when one's right there and you
can't scoop it up in a net, or get your line out fast enough—
like what always used to happen when I was a kid fishing.
Suddenly a school of mackerel or blues would be thick beneath us,
and all it needed to get one or twenty was to put the right-sized hook
and an eel over the side and bang bang, just like that—a boatful.
Sometimes I guess I was quick enough, but more often than not
I blew it, napping or sneaking Oreos, an apple, down below
when everyone else got a hit. By the time I'd found my rod,
others had reeled their tackle in, heavy and shaking with hungry,
angry muscle that flapped and whanged on the deck.
The only way I'd catch anything would be trolling later,
heading home, while big gulls worked in the air astern,
the sea like shiny tiles, that sweet fish oil smell everywhere.

Seasonal

Almost Labor Day again.
Woodpecker on old vine startled by quarrelsome sparrows
flies off into juniper bush. He makes no sound in leaving
unlike local kingfishers who keep machinegun chatter
rattling as they loop down to feast on flashing smelt.

I might have nothing to say.
At 70 no pictures to show or any books with candyass
covers showing cities on fire and luscious blondes sucking
gun barrels as might have been my achievement my life's
first inkling of greatness to come working in anonymity
until my breakthrough my picture in *Times Book Review*.

I always knew he'd be great
she might say. When we were in sixth grade he helped
me with my homework. And his imagination! Really no
end to it! And that part is true. If I have nothing it is not
because I am just a journeyman hack like those sparrows.

Another ruthless kingfisher
soaring hunting hiding swooping feasting
endlessly chattering even when perched. Keep watch.
Listen hard as if you were in a forest. Stay alert open
tracking. List all birds you see sounds you hear. There is life
and danger all around you. Be quiet and look. You will hear
cities burn down see a blonde put your gun between her lips.

Tashlich Service

All those sins are floating out on the lake to sink
like leaves growing soft and spidery in the water.
With any luck they'll be gone by tomorrow morning.
Along an upper road's edge the 6 of Spades facedown
on grass and cinders with the 2 of Clubs and 10
of Diamonds, tossed perhaps from a rusting Chevy,
sitting low on its rear suspension, making a rattle
like an old outboard being revved in a steel barrel
to flush out summer's grime before the off-season.

That car or pickup or whatever was driven maybe
by someone called Art, whose entire name is still
lying muddied on a short, stern, printed letter also
possibly thrown out the window, wherein a law firm
in Albany gives our boy the option of paying his debt
or having his bank account and property attached.
Art's sins reside here now, under a pine with cement
and rusty farm stuff throttled in ground vetch—
indissoluble markers for us all on a warm fall day.

He contemplates his fall garden

I range around these days,
looking for what withers, or might,
next. There are so many quiet flowers
without support any longer in this world.
I am often scared in autumn, but try to stay
informal, like a squash or cabbage—present
without half trying. Not yet old,
avoiding bad illness or infirmity,
I grow slower—more inside than out.
For this, tired, I am thankful.

Summer's still loose in the air, though,
upsetting those who deal with each year
like prime real estate. Their categorizing
is serious, troublesome. As for me,
flighty as milkweed, but *sans legerdemain*,
plump, I rise more curious each morning,
rhetoric sharper than a late radish.

Geese flying

Their hearts know nothing.
Earth's magnetic lines direct them,
or the sun, or stars—perhaps all these.
Below, landmarks of their way: hills, ponds,
signs of men where they've worked, and, working,
looked up and thought, "What we do with this journey
is only ours and no other's. Soon we too will head south
toward warmth, careful of the space around us,
minding our place in the larger pattern,
letting the rhythm move us on
as much as might any wing,
or shivering desire."

On the scaffold

The sky clears like a gunshot
after two days of rain. He wants to find
new ways to say what has been said before
on such changes. His coat luffs in the air.
It is French—brown canvas with a shoulder cape—
wrong for hard weather, boasting more than it can do.
A cloudbank surges toward him. One brief moth spirals
across its face. All the leaves veer off, pleading.
And now, smooth, black, impervious,
comes that executioner wind.

Too late

The steps no longer lead back up like Escher's
toward the beginning. His sight grows watery
as clouds thicken and grow dark, wind pesters.
A clutch of leaves outside flips a little—some
whiff of breeze beside the cove—he thinks
he sees a bird before bright flickers at edges
of his vision merge to a yellow plane again,
and trees become shapeless in slanted rain.
He pants as if suffocated under invisible billows
of stone. Squally swirls on autumn tide's surface
blow across slate gray shine and marsh grass.
When he wakes tomorrow, he will be alone,
frightened, and no one will offer him solace.

November changes

Sparrows go slantwise across the street.
Last shreds of leaves zip downwind.
And a heavy breeze it is, straight out
of the west-northwest, everything
chilling off where it gusts and whirls.
Along the horizon that stretches out
just this side of a second continental lift,
the sky's bright and spreading this way,
bare trunks red in the sun's sudden blaze.
I wonder how to say what needs saying
and how to make another start when
my whole window is filled with scud
flying like those leaves due east.
Words would be snatched and hurled
along out into the Atlantic, its roar
growing with the gale. Be glad
you're not at sea now, I think,
where waves rise up to smack against
men's wishes, sweeping boats off
course as if they were small sparrows
trying to get safely from here to there.

Approaching Solstice

Cold panes moist inside cut by clear lines
where air rushes out. Doors not matching jambs,
one flue broken, open, unhinged. Mail slot stuck.
His son swears at him, won't leave his room.
A friend complains, "They should have crucified
now, not Easter. It's the right weather for it."
He reads that Finns call this "Dead Time"
in *syystalvi*, winter's first stage.

On Friday night a ring around the moon
suggests to him Diana as Byzantine saint—
or the Light Itself in gold mosaic,
high-domed, set with lapis lazuli,
a solid halo around the centered disk.
He finds a place where one streetlight
makes shadows on asphalt over other leaf
outlines traced in soot days ago. Two seasons
there—one a skeleton, another still shaking
and curled, like a fish, striving to fit
those older patterns in an evening breeze.

Snow, hidden in the moon's ring,
comes on Saturday, catching maples unprepared,
breaking off low branches still leafed out.
In other centuries, useful firewood—
a grove's floor opened up for new growth.
Now just clutter on pavement gathered up
by thirteen city men in two trucks
and a noisy orange scoop ringing its Angelus

when it backs, elevates a load of muck,
and bows with screams of metal on metal,
incense of diesel in the air, cruciform mud.

But Sunday brings a wonderful surprise.
Whatever storm computers guaranteed
has missed completely. There's a northwest wind—
cool aftermath of someone else's gale.
He drives his son to a place they've always loved—
a granite spearhead thrust aggressively into wind
from Maine, the Maritimes, the Pole itself. Rocks
everywhere, split off by Finnish quarrymen
who worked the pit here once, sending granite
south by barge to Boston or New York for curbs
or for foundation stones. At ocean's edge, sun
behind them shoots their shadows out (his son's
hooded, hovering on the waves' huge swells).

Then great Poseidon's house-high stallion rears,
the boy's delighted yell lost in water's roar—
visible Earthshaker! pillar of white! curved shock!
Their shadows hurtle back, are gathered in,
the god's own breath prismatic turbulence
in their celebrant mouths, all salt and ecstasy.

On the sea toward Maine, a low flight of birds
curls suddenly above the dark, wings white,
many as one, moving freely, and disappears.

This season

We do not know each other well until winter
draws us closer. There is food and wine, fires
to sit beside. Someone plays old songs on a piano.
We think in bright bursts about times long gone
and remember fiercely that joy and expectation
we took for granted. Now it's on to another place,
another tune, laughter, merriment, new words,
coming quickly and leaving, like electric trains
in a store window, like wonderful days we hoped
would come quickly and stay with us forever.
We turn to each other and sing our hearts' wishes.

Leaving that year behind

(12.31.01)

In the meadow there is black ice around clumps of grass
where the melting began, and stymied by night's cold stopped.
As turf warms again there are distant rifle snaps of action
and water moves like blood under brittle crusts that lace
out in wires disappearing as winter's white sun rises.

Near the housecorner by that scruffy juniper all blued out
with berries there is noise whenever wind quickens
that sounds like a child moaning and crying inconsolably.
What is to be done? How will I die? No one can help me.
This rises and fades to silence. Branches scrape the window.

I'm so glad you were knitting that beautiful afghan today.
There are colors in it that make spring seem not so far off
we can't manage to get through this. I want to go to a street fair
where the wailing and disappearance are only dreams or fears
still unrealized—where the dear dead sing again and dance.

Tomorrow we start over. We promise ourselves to become new.
In the meadow though and near the house there will still be
nightmarish moments nothing can stop not even conscious effort
in an absolute spring to come when leaves unroll, blackbirds call
and sweet breezes make it all all right again just for the moment.

PEOPLE

Grolier tape

*One minute in the mind of Gordon Cairnie is worth
all the crap that's been written about American
poetry and poets, and most of the poems, too.* Anon.

Books, books, books. You either come in or go out. If it's not on the
shelf, I don't have it. Never heard of him. Who? No textbooks. Can't
you read? Damned browsers. Wear out my books. You just missed
what's-his-name. Black Horse Ale? Don't mind if I do. Something you
should see. It's there on the table someplace. Eh? That's my lunch.
Forgot my teeth. Got today's *Times*, though. He was in here once,
that feller what's-his-name. It'll come to me. Save that envelope.
Got to pump ship. No smoking. Shut the door. Cute little thing.
Poor old Horace Reynolds. Good old vodka. The First War. Divinity
Hall. Landscape architecture. *That* bastard! There is a fountain filled
with blood. My God! The old days. Aiken liked a martini. Ezra. I was
there once. It's here someplace. Coaticook. Potato bug inspector.
Ontario Agricultural College. In Guelph. Same as Galbraith. Deaf as a
post. I don't know a thing about it. Amazing Grace. Rock of Ages. I'll
take the bus. An old fart like me. Yes, of course I did. Yes. Goodbye.
Goodbye. Yes, I will. Yes. Yes, I will. Yes. Goodbye, goodbye,
goodbye. GOODBYE.

Getting through it

I confess to taking pain-killers—two so far today.
Makes me a little woozy, but absence of sharp
stabs in my lower back and stinging tightness
in glutes and hams is worth a few dulled moments
and an occasional error in thought or speech.
Spurred to memory by Orlovsky's death in Vermont,
I revisit moments fifty years old, naïvèté then
hanging out of my pants, imagining bright ideas
I hadn't had yet and fucking never done with girls
I'd never meet. True, I did get Peter's autograph,
and Ginsberg's twice, Corso's and Olson's too there
in a bookstore on a day in dull winter, but what
did I do after that? Carried their names to Europe
in a canvas pannier on the back of an old motorcycle
I bought in London with $400 earned washing cars
in a gas station on Mass. Avenue so the magazine
they'd signed was all scuffed and dogeared
and the only sex all summer was with a ditzy painter
from Mount Holyoke staying in a dorm in Copenhagen
whence I was ejected at dawn by a Danish guy
with glasses who looked like someone I knew in school.
Did any of that pass even then for illumination—
a state I craved, combing my hair like Rimbaud's?

Industrious Landscape

G. G.

I would just mention the clearing away of snow
and other digging we have done together,
startling rectangles emerging from white fields—
plenty of room now for what is to come.

In this weather days here begin harshly.
We straggle out cursing in steam
to rebreak soil soft last night
and heat brittle engines.

Then we have visions of women,
nude on a beach, turning gold,
while laughing children play in waves,
and as we dig, we warm.

Spring at Bear Mountain

April is tolling him on.
Snow rots on the ground,
ascending souls wheeze across his roof.
The birches are diseased, bent
in uncomfortable arches, smashed
as if an avalanche had run them down.
Road stones sluice a muddy dribble.

He braved the morning, walked
the upper pasture, daring
omnivorous Spring to follow.
Deers' nests under Scotch pine,
last night's spoor scattered
near the field's melting edge.
Childish and isolated,
impressionable, on unfamiliar ground,
he lay in one of those hollows
thinking of environmental ruin,
lost his nerve and train of thought,
and went back down, wet and self-conscious,
not a deer at all.

He's fussed with books and paper,
deskbound since noon, fighting off
diarrhea from greasy fries, picking
at some remnants of his conscience.
His compass of desire's shrunk.
He addresses his fantasy, "I wish
you'd come and slide your pants off."
There is no response. He goes to sleep.

Dear Joe Kennedy

If meter's mastered in a line so plain,
does that reduce or add to all our pain?
Vocabulary's narcissism, wit,
can't camouflage a poet who's a nit.
Gold hair in mirror's glass reflects in gold
"Good morning to the day," and soon, "Grown old!"
And while this may've been adequate for Possum,
one can't deny that Time may doublecross him.
Yea, nonetheless, I list among my pleasures,
you, yours, a dying cadence, *Counter/Measures*.

The work-out

I am dressed in my old grey running suit.
I have a towel for sweat and a jockstrap
because my fear is great. I will myself

out onto the track to join you,
hurdling and sprinting the countryside,
because you can not wait for me.

I envy your directness and speed—
I bet you were the fastest runner
in the sixth grade—and your control!

You move right along the blade
of your slicing vision.
I must accept the limits

of a slower pace. I'm in it
for distance—no special
regimens or diet, thank you,

just a normal growth. No breakthroughs.
You with your pounding, nervous strength,
committed to great leaps and deep breaths,

bolt out, driven by laughing
or crying. Your exertion makes me gasp.
But I long for your pace—

no doubts, no hesitation, just
the plunge forward, the awful
crashing and surging of the new.

Bloodlines

M.

If your mother's folks came from Sandusky,
you would know about screened porches
on the lakeshore, where the junebugs
are not brown and hard, but gauze-winged,
dying in huge, light clouds, your first reasons
to think as a serious child about how suddenly
these—all creatures—are suddenly not alive,
and you would know things are not forever
when you went to sleep in the summer.

If your mother's folks came from Adelaide,
that hill-ringed city, you would grow up
listening to stories of the Outback,
knowing about the kookaburra long before
you ever saw one, thinking in childhood
how alone and far she and you were now
from a wonderful place that smelled always
of eucalyptus, flowering lilli pilli, the sea,
where people just got up one morning and left.

Forgiven at forty

J. T.

I see the lost poet carried upstairs
by one large shape, down by another, smiling,
among the easiest talkers ever, and eager!
so fucking thirsty! half cocked on old secrets.

Was it that your verse just wowed folks?
Hell, I don't know—sounded fine to me,
convolved in the middle of a silly life,
presenting books as birchrods to masochists.

Oh my, what times in streets or bars at night
in those days, goosing lumpy matrons with poems.
But I hear Irby, poppin' and snappin' in Lawrence,
sing, "Roll up my trousers and peel me a peach."

Now at last that I miss you I want to ask
(given this fine occasion and all)
Is Kansas City holy still? and
How'd you really like them flowers, honey?

For Carl Woods

(d. 1979)

What he taught grows rarer with his going—
always be surprised, open to possibilities,
don't dare pass a place, object, event without dreaming it
into otherness. He never heard a story or a poem
he didn't interrupt, breathless, rushing
toward its outcome, taken over, awed
by the process of telling, not by words.
Demonstrating a guitar to friends, he missed
his fingering, impatient to make whole songs.

Along the road, picking up paper like jewelry,
he lost himself, floated out toward trees,
put his mind into birds or shells, forgetting
suddenly his place, all places, his name.

To be called the name of many trees at once
was his undoing, answering as he did, all blind
and open, each one—as if a member of his own
immediate family were there, or his dead wife.

Exclaiming to God, he never made things out,
could not have known the car or truck, failed
to sense that it was other than his own, no
extension of himself, no little breeze rising behind.

He surely heard instead amazing fugues,
perhaps appraised all notes in one moment,
caught the sound of every drop in a ground swell
from the Pacific, rumbling up near Santa Barbara.
And, perfectly at home among Vivaldi's chords,
he sang one last, wondering, astonished poem.

Bodybuilder

He is pulling blood in,
trying to be strong in the mirror.
The word gives him trouble
and he pushes it away, wondering,
what will come now? who will come?
All his adventures are in his mind.
The large muscles serve no one.
He dreams of Austria and hopes
to be a policeman. He would like
to lift the roof off his mother's house.
He would like to be perfectly alone.
He would like to be a boulder.
He would like to hold everything,
just as it is, forever.

Holderness

G.T.B.

This his own voice talking of another fresh egg,
of stones in the pond like horses' backs,
who are grazing on a pasture's slope,
dark stones against the green,
while thin waists, thin hips, slide
across his mind, and kids out the window chant
"fingerpaint fingerpaint" atonal, complacent
in the pliable air. Leaves turn over, show white.
Those children outside hum like crickets who sing
mindlessly, like children during an afternoon
in September at his cousin's house in New Hampshire
when summer breaks at last. The egg is quite perfect.
Waist, hips roll toward him, crows call,
swallows grow silent as all in this world
wait for storm, for fall's fault line,
for an end to this their "one fine summer."
Sheep raise random hosannahs in the ripe haze.

Dream Beach

K.

Noon and there's a greenhead in the kitchen.
"You ought to make a note of that,"
his friend enjoins, curious, impatient,

boiling water in a frypan for tea.
There is a space above the screen door
through which said fly did come.

Tide goes out below. Behind those dunes
is marsh where greenheads breed. It rains
now—huge drops making shadows on sand.

Three kids, their dog like Buster's Tige,
come past, heading home. They want to chunk
bottles in some trashcans by the windbreak.

They look up, ask, are throwing, all at once,
have no interest in an answer. Glass
bounds on sand, scatters rain's shadows.

There is a preachment of starlings' voices
in the rising squall. He dances, bareheaded,
spinning in windy gusts, and hollers,

"Young boys, best trundle your asses
up that hillside in one quick hurry!"
His friend offers commentary—

"The men appropriate swift feet, winged feet.
They climb and pass the boys, as if on horses
somewhere in Kansas. They turn and wait."

COMPLEXITIES

Mirage

A crow dances down the corn,
our pride and labor.
His blind eye devours sunlight,
ignores the land's struggle
against something careless
and sharp.

Our road shrugs up blisters.
The crow arcs his beak
and scythes among the rows.

Dream of war

All through this smoky morning,
friends scatter to their places by the wall
with signs, flags, flowers, handkerchiefs.
Columns unroll from gates like carpets
kicked out in all directions. This way
for millenia now—"Goodbye. I love you."

Ominous regiments ease down valleys,
noiseless triremes without oars or sails.
Steel plows gouge up riverbeds, shear
rock, seal caves, leave hands outlined
on walls in astonished gestures. Remnants
of the battle freeze in each cascade.

Armies unravel slowly. Each hour
broken bodies curl up beside roads—
canteens on embankments, helmets under bushes,
swords, bags, bonesplinters,
an empty wheelbarrow, rifles, crutches,
traces of a bloody passage in dim light.
A face shows above stones
beneath clear ice, its jaw thrust up,
eyes set, compelled, mirroring your own.

Shoichi

"No fault—to side with what was weak in me."

Guam, where the American day begins, is the expected honey-
moon site of SHOICHI YOKOI, a former Japanese Army sergeant,
and Miss MIHOKO HATASHIN, who are scheduled to be
married. If anyone knows the attractions of the small Pacific isle,
it should be the 57-year-old Mr. Yokoi. In January, he was the last
Japanese soldier, to date, to surrender after World War II. He was
discovered after hiding for 28 years in the Guam jungles, defeated
but uninformed. After their first three dates, the 44-year-old Miss
Hatashin said, "We can now communicate with each other by eyes,
though we don't talk to each other much."

The New York Times
September 30, 1972

Here is Shoichi   on Guam
"where the American day begins."
We've pushed it that far
trying to lock in on the real
pushing West always.
Shoichi Yokoi, Sergeant
for several lifetimes   Japanese
Guamaian   knowing terrain so well
he was a changing letter on the landscape
slipping for 28 years along dark coordinates.
A plumb bob hanging at interstice Guam
in his century.

Shoichi repatriate kissing tarmac   weeping empire's death
with numb memories of jungle flame   surprising high bark
of grenades   sounds all day of bullets never fired
in a rainforest full of invisible enemies
primed to kill a careless man   or one disloyal.
Loyalty, intelligence, neatness all one stratagem—
"It is with much embarrassment that I have returned alive."

51

Moving always by night he made footprints
villagers saw and reported to patrols   these coming
less and less frequently   less and less interested
hardly anymore believing that it might be more than a drunk
or a petty thief   or a lover
coming home too late to explain.
Villages have such tracks. Shoichi's footprints not unique.
Only the fact of his 28 years unseen
makes us chary of casual explanations.

A soldier's rituals carried out alone
the Emperor remembered daily   also dead friends
ancestors and early teachings.
Guam becomes one's family.
Those things mean most that are inanimate
kept safe by order and devotion   the large tree
a vine sending tendrils out   these above suspicion
single of purpose   always clean   moving at night.

Engaged after nine months in the homeland
married to the shy and sidelong Mihoko Hatashin
who spoke for them   *"We can now communicate with each
other by eyes though we don't talk
to each other much."*

The honeymoon: Guam again by plane
Shoichi tense on landing   seeing the island through glasses
for the first time since his twenties.
Government Jeep   barking dogs   villagers by now inventing

whole lost battalions   selling spent cartridges
the number of dawn footprints up by a third this year.
From road's end they hike to his shelter   she peeps
into caves   wonders   by eyes   how he managed
worries at the sight of him among the vines.
Into his clearing   now in mortal grapple with jungle
gathered straw matted under mud
spiders' slings where hammocks hung
one last book bored out before he could return.
Mihoko reaches eyes and unfamiliar hands   Yokoi's
glasses off   no way to talk   face unknown.
He blows air out like a man spitting hot soup
runs to a large tree beside the ledge his burrow's in
throws his arms around   caressing   growing on its trunk
then is still and neat while he takes his orders for the night.

Making a play

No one knows my name here,
but your motion
and my slowness
ensure collision.
Kneedeep in the dust
I am unable to move.

Bounding
hellbent
you.

Rooted me.

You lengthen my anticipation,
hesitating there,
right
on the edge
of your green kingdom,
before daring mine.

Mated

We have one thing
(the fan begins to whirl, I've turned it on)
its shape distinct, singing in easy tension
like a sprinter's sinews or a sawblade,
confident among old pines.
For you the equipoise of flight returning
always to pursuit. For me the promise
of an edged coin spinning. Now
watch silently the burning air.

In Aquarius

You were there when I woke up this morning
dancing the twostep with me
round and round together
my hand on your hip
round and round
twin stars in frantic orbits
an oil rig's bit boring down
the center pole of a merry-go-round
biting through the cement of its foundation
carrying all the animals below the water level.

But our dance thrusts us up like whirlybirds
or bullets   our spin imparted by springs
and barrels that burst us out
or launching pads
our spin and roll controlled
by distant monitors' bodiless voices
calling out numbers in mysterious sequences:

(Pi)

———
— —
— —
———
— —
———

which "shows a fire that breaks out of the secret
depths of the earth and, blazing up, illuminates
and beautifies the mountain, the heavenly heights.
Grace—beauty of form—is necessary in any union

if it is to be well ordered and pleasing
rather than disordered and chaotic. . . .
By contemplating the forms existing in the heavens
we come to understand time and its changing demands."
"Thus," it continues, this voice, "does the superior man
proceed when clearing up current affairs. But
he dare not decide controversial issues in this way."
O, our spin continues unabating.
Then the voice says—now hear this and believe—
that "form is to be considered only as a result
and attribute of content." What spins us is ourselves
our fantasies
ourselves coming   as if on wings.

In this whirling pitching craft
blessed to circle the goal
but destined—graceful and moist—never to land
we dance. Poor thrumming spindles on a dark field
taking our chances with a simple trust. No blame.
No telling if the dance will stop, or when.
Don't want it to but must be circumspect.
Should conserve power.
Almost out of oxygen.

[The text of this commentary does not seem to be intact.]

He undergoes a peculiar metamorphosis

She's like the moon—at perigee his tides
are out of whack, his coasts tormented.
What was one place is called another,
farther in or out than on the charts
or in old stories. He rents a plane
and flies up in the evening to observe
as one might an eclipse, or hurricane,
or nine planets in a perfect line.
She shines so hard the engines falter
and he slips into a comet's orbit, is gone
for seven years.
                        When he returns
he lands on her dark side (she all unwary),
puts his hands over her face from behind,
and asks for his names back, and places.
She has a voice like strong bright wires
suspending graceful weights in the wind.
She gives him an amulet made from her hair.
He wears it and sleeps for the first time
since she woke him with sounds of water.
He dreams of hands clapping, music behind curtains,
and birds with cries like children playing tag.
He breakfasts on plates of wildflowers and berries.
When he goes to work, the whole landscape is blue,
made of some delicate ceramic, only the hills glazed,
and the sea, and parts of certain trees and roads.
His desk is made of round black stones, his shirt
of ivy, his paper and thinking are the moon.

He revises his life

Everybody worries over summer storms—
that in the general scramble, their things
will get trampled, soaked, forgotten, lost.
In the sudden, shifting breeze, he tries
to remember the phrases that bring sleep
and quash the panic in his lower gut.

When I was little, living in the country
west of Boston with my mother during the war,
all alone (my father in North Africa),
the hired man next door, a refugee
named Harlan, who put me on a black pony
and led me around the pasture, one morning,
while the dogs barked, died.
My mother told me she had sat by his bed,
and he was very sick and went to sleep forever.
She brought me something to remember him—
a small yellow pitcher with a black handle,
white inside, with a line of black on the rim,
and on the unglazed bottom, in a little circle,
Made in Czecho-Slovakia—which I have kept.
Though chipped, it has not been broken, and seems
as dear to me now as anything I own.

He dreams on the screened porch
while the lighthouse turns and turns
between tumbled granite and dark water.
"I am a dancer," she sings,
"who may not be followed."
She executes difficult leaps and spins,
graceful extensions of her smooth limbs,
all down a long rail—moments of dark wood,

of gleaming brass, circles of her arms,
white when raised, mirrored forever in corners.
He can't remember what this is like,
must wake to keep the small vessel of his love
from breaking, would conceal himself, silent,
in spare, shadowed interiors of summer houses
where he once slept well, heard nothing,
so that threats in the skirmishing wind,
the sprinting, dancing rain, might blow over,
so there might be no rushing, no turning,
no darkness, no memories of absence.

He asks her out

Love, let's drive to Wichita together.
Des Moines, my soul, Grand Forks or Dallas.
We'll string it out, share fatigue, food, cash, bed,
cruise, meander, taking time to hear the wires,
barely visible, singing in darkness beside us.

The parts all match, the metal's furbished.
Not even half a road to pass on, but he's ready.
He maneuvers, dancing gravely at his wheel,
until the curves end and clean, flat asphalt
starts to whinny underneath his beautiful machine.

The radio plays two stations. One they've passed,
the other out ahead—simultaneous, overlapped,
fading in and out as the land unfolds, twisted
edge to edge by weather and topography. Jittery,
curious, she listens to a priest say Hail Marys
behind surging blisters of rock and chatter.
The storm in her head is bright yellow.

Angle of Incidence

Shared passion for the indirect
compels them—her pulling back
from the flat of saying what
would pierce the tension, as though
she saw there some failed dream,
some pain, some mirror, crying.

She will visit Japan instead,
she will love a stone, a jar,
a tree, young men, will look
(anywhere) off dead center
while he agitates their silence,
laying, in full knowledge, himself open.

That one, she says, is "naïve
as rain." Someone else "will
not say where he stands."
Her sister "is heartbroken."

These are skillful caroms, angles
around what once she dared
to say in a car on her way
to an airport through her own
vast untidy city without edges.

It is by refraction, her game,
that he will have to move.
"If you won't come in," he might call
to her, "I will carry you."
He would not mean this—though
the suggestion slips easily enough
between one surface and another.

Cadences of desire

It is here that he proposes to her—
over great distance, a doll falling
out of a canvas bag as he carries his boy
into a dark cottage on a deadend dirt road
in the country. It is 9:30 Labor Day evening,
summer's end, and everyone is friendly, high
enough for kindness and to sing as needed
to children during dinner as they wander
through the house. What matters, though,
as the tape unwinds later in his car, as he
hears "Coyote" on a highway in Vermont,
is that nothing heals, nothing moves
forward as it once did. Stillness
in the country   insects   stars.

Love lyric in Santa Monica

There is this glass-sided building burning
behind me with the fire of a sun going down.
At the same time a full February moon, there,
like a huge soft streetlight just switched on,
a full globe between palm trees and a spire,
stopped in the evening sky, breathing almost.

So what more can I say to make you see
how this all felt when it started, how
I suddenly came across my life laid out
like clean, sweet clothes on a square table
in the corner of your room, with morning light
flowing in through high windows as you turned?

He is part of a Möbius strip

Then she told him the story of the story
that never happened between them, before
it was never to come true, or before
she discovered that it was just a story,
never what was going to be, before
what was not to happen between them
had not happened, as she had still
thought it might, in her story.

Later she believed that what had never
happened might be as true as if it had.
Then she discovered that it just might
be going to happen later, or be a story
still to come, if she told him her thought.

He creates a pattern for chaos

"Not without imagination," is what he says to her,
 speaking of secrets or the future, possibly a lie.
 Talk moves between them like an old rope
 through a greased pulley, now heavy, now eased.
 She ponders new costumes for old roles.
 He putters, nods off in the dim light, puzzled
 by the smoothness of it, the swift glide of knowing
 what he knows she knows, troubled by small fears.

 Trailing behind as she carries incense to her room,
 he grunts, climbs stairs in the late afternoon light.
 He is exhausted suddenly by the effort of holding on.
 He imagines poplars by a river, orange tiled roofs.
 He imagines his own death by suffocation,
 sees his face, ecstatic, when the breathing stops.

Abandoned

Don't worry be happy they write,
climbing those Sierra passes.
But he's dreaming of making love
to a mountainous lady, booted,
her nipples like medals, bouncing
around, a killer, all over him.
This sex, he thinks, is like being
hacked by four slowmotion knights
in silk nightgowns over chainmail vests,
tasseled selvages all gobbeted.

Fragments

Parchment leaf   black twig   drizzle
my father trying to die jaundiced skin
tear ducts stuck open.

Sixteen years later
same bed my mother follows   it takes
so long she said.

Anniversary

A year past her death my watch went haywire,
not the hours but the days and dates—jumping
or not to their proper spots sometime in the night
as intended. I believe she may have gotten a kick
out of that, floating beyond time, but just able
to make out what happens here, as from her chair
by the fireplace, bright little eyes dimmed behind
thick glasses that never enabled her to see well—
the one loss she lamented over and over until
those who loved her got angry and scolded.
Maybe my ailing watch, readable but unreliable,
is her revenge for cross words then. She knows,
though, that her carriage clock still ticks away,
losing or gaining time and never exact
for more than one day. With time wobbly,
she could always leave for something early,
dragging children along, fearing lateness.
It is never polite to be late, she taught—never.
She died early in the morning, after a long,
ritual withdrawal from food. A little water,
no food. None. Her hands grew clawlike.
Are you comfortable, I asked, watching the time.
Fairly, she said, eyes shut, sly smile (dry humor
much favored), her clock ticking on the bureau,
odors of cologne, clean sheets, age.

Stone boat

Contemplating his father's death, his mother's illness,
he found he understood nothing, stopped, skirted
all that, took up instead a rope attached to a sledge
loaded with granite blocks, a "stone boat," spat
on his hands and started to heave, just to be pulling it—
to see how far he'd get before he, too, faltered.
Behind, whispering, groaning through the grass,
the sledge moved—a juggernaut in field or woods,
furrowing up turf, hedgerows, saplings—crushing
its way at a pace so slow it seemed half a life
before the entire bulk went past, half a life.

Possibly he will put soon the hawser, wrapped with tape
around its cut end to stop hemp's splay, down. Possibly
he cannot, would not if he could, and will keep placing
heavily the balls of his soles against earth's slope,
or sometimes his heels, his curled toes, feet sometimes
laid almost over on ankles from that weight behind,
treadmill soil curling always away beneath him.

Desire that stings the heart

It was nothing intentional—nothing
like sculpture, for instance,
or a photograph of a small boy laughing.
When it had begun, there was no way of telling,
no catch in a hand's movement, or hesitation
in a word in the throat.

Instead it seemed as though rain
fell at a different angle
because the breeze had shifted,
or as if they were shadows on a wall,
and their bodies floated together, apart,
as the light behind them moved a little.

The pain of its actual happening

What belongs to us both we can really just
sort out over time, she says. Meanwhile,
a ball has been hit to left centerfield
on a long parabola. It turns out to be made
of glass, with a huge teardrop of air inside,
like honey in a jar. Now it is curving down,
about to reach him. How was it hit so hard
without breaking? He has a long time to think.
The whole scene seems like a frame
in a comic book. The air is painted
WHOOSH to show the velocity of its approach,
but the ball just hangs there, teasing him,
outwaiting gravity, young in the air forever.

Closing down in Connecticut

      L.

Today the geese seem scarcely to grow smaller
before they disappear beyond some maple trees
across a pond. This has perhaps to do with the size
of their bodies relative to the speed and regularity
of their wings. Only their crying diminishes
in the thin cold, fading beneath his tires' psalms
on wet pavement, the rattle of loose shades,
a careless woman's bent spring of a laugh.

This is a time of going away—no clear colors left,
no instance even of a single leaf's drop.
The effect is one of gradual absence,
of a departure during which nothing alters
until it has, indeed, gone entirely away,
and what was known until now is now unknown.

Transparency

When the sun is finally up, it will be as though
the person in the pictures you still have of him
had just yellowed out—faded away altogether.
If he were holding up a tiny fish on the beach,
for instance, it would float motionless before you,
a small notch like a crosshair on the horizon.
Or if your arm were around his shoulder
as you walked back up Ocean Avenue, hip
to hip, you would seem to be smiling
at the curve of your bicep, at your hand.
In the place where he stood in your kitchen,
a serrated knife has sliced an orange all on its own,
precisely down the middle. The two halves still touch.
And under the big palm in your back yard, you hang up
a T-shirt, dark eyes wide, gesturing to a metal chair
on which a towel dries. How can this be?
Not so much as an edge. No words. No heft.
Nothing that leaves a shadow on venetian blinds
in his hotel room near the beach. Yet some whisper,
some stir in the morning, gives an impression of him
turning, very near, toward you and away again.

Tinnitus

It used to come in the first of morning, lightly,
like the touch of felted wood on taut wire,
exact as a tuner's fork—
that small, single, worrisome note.
And he would stand in the shower, listening,
guessing this was tinnitus,
an early sign of deafness or perhaps this time
just distraction, going nuts.

The hiss and gurgle of water, then a telephone
sound. Indeed, he several times leapt out,
soaking floor and carpet, to answer no one,
the shock to no effect, the sound quite gone,
him knowing, crazy in the chill air,
that it was false, part of a false moment,
half dream. Still he heard it quaver
and fought instinct, turning his face
into spray, breathing wet heat in
with head down so as to, he explained,
clear his tubes.

It was ringing, not ringing, ringing,
that one clear then absent sound he heard,
analogous perhaps to amputation when the limb
still aches. What heals it (and it heals)
is time spent hearing nothing,
and the growing sureness that the mind wins,
that alone he is whole and complete, able even
in the steam to learn and sing his own ancient
soaring sweet familial songs.

Observations from a rented space

Two chairs tilt seat to seat, arm to arm,
like lovers, bodies frozen in intimate exchange.
Perhaps they whisper innocuous lies about summer
or winter. One maybe says, "I'm tired of this."
The other replies with a question about fidelity,
indistinctly, words lost in a scuffle of leaves.

This happens while the light starts to slide away.
Two floors up, a single, drying plant stares out—
a stem, thin, green, in a pot wrapped with foil,
aloof, attenuated, like a painted stick, or one
of Giacometti's starved bronze knights seen long ago
on someone's hall table in Chicago.

The threat of loss, of losing ground, is present
in all he sees or feels—in the wind, the trees,
his room, the way he makes his bed, writes letters,
is unable, looking out on broken stairs festooned
with white twine at those chairs, to hold her clearly
in his thoughts for longer than a chestnut's fall.

Musings of her fancy man

    B.

Princeton

Here in New Jersey high far planes
going into Newark blend faint jet noise
with radios from cars beyond her fence.
It is warm spring at last, good to walk
through a garden's evening dream, calmed
by flagstone geometry, by flowers, by ideas,
by the certainty of home: lilacs and dogwoods
in pencilled rain. What matters most is here,
filled with long, sweet echoes of promise.

Wellfleet

"Didn't those mosquitoes come down like
the Luftwaffe?" she asks, slapping
at her perfect ankles while Madonna
sings a song about spanking, teenage sexy,
over two small speakers on the mantelpiece.
Off to the east, beyond gray wooden railings,
and even further than the edge of the pond
his son drew before supper, last whorls
of a hurricane boom up on the outer beach.

In some idiocy of the day's late morning heat
he disgraced himself and earned a lesson
in acceptance of rebuke from her, losing
everything for a moment when, cramps
screwing his stomach, he thought her gripe
was with him—his fathering or something—
the parts he suddenly thought himself,

in wild whirls, hopeless at. Heavy with anger
in the overcast afternoon, he finally heard
his honor lashed. He took a walk, questioned
himself, reality, motives, the whole *histoire*,
then pushed, guts in a knot, one thought after
another, beyond whatever it was in her head,
to try to make the memories right in his own.

Which came first, they wondered later, and what
could either one count on taking away from this?
They drove home tired, and diddled about,
salving themselves in little chores. When the sun
bloomed again, the air cleared and he took a picture
of soaring gulls in his mind's lens, exposure perfect.

Skating

We wobble and scoot heroically, we glide
in long curls through the rink's chill bright air,
smooth and steady on our blades' edges.

This sporting is no one's natural mode.
Our strength lies in our good intention only.
We put on willpower, discipline, set out,
laced tight, counterclockwise, each turn
moving under us as if completion
could produce a sudden accolade,
loving, welcome bursts from a home crowd.

The sounds we make are like some kiss or word
still unformed. A shadow curls forward, a wave
on cloudy smoothness, ice in small showers
up and out, while we two slide together,
with flickering sidelong looks, around
and around,
forever.

PLACES

Blurry in Manhattan

Not being farsighted enough there is a limit
to what new glasses can do for him in the city.
Bifocalled he cannot see his feet properly
on down escalators, buildings three blocks away
are indistinct, everything darker than usual.
On rain-glazed asphalt, faint tracks of a man
walking ahead on his soles' outsides fade
as he follows them carefully along. Yet he sees
at lunch later clearly enough deathmask madeup
women clustered at a near table shriek weddings,
concerts, kitchens. Seated, he can hear disembodied
whacks of piled crockery somewhere, then clunk
clunk of a loose manhole cover. Indistinct forms
are everywhere around him as if he inhabited
a huge room, altogether separate from the world.
Behind lenses no earthly way to set matters right.

Late again walking west

Because Manhattan's avenues fan up
from its dagger tip, addresses are hard to find.
The way to figure it, a cabbie once explained,
is simple enough to relearn every time: no grid.
I zap across town, suited, briefcased, late.
Mattawan on a truck cab's open door,
Belasco Theater, Paradise Restaurant.
Time To Think About Eternity! it says on a wall,
and on a Chevy's bumper, Keep It Simple.

 Man in a plaid jacket, plaid shirt, green pants,
shouts. He works hard for his money! his eyes dead
outside the Zona Rosa Café, weaving to his left.
You should respect him! he calls to two girls,
to bearded diamond merchant saints in black
hurrying past. You should, you should!
he weeps, veering off, laying his own grid
upon the world he sees, asking only that it might
take him as he is, on a Midtown street this afternoon.

Outdoor living

End of city and Lefrak buildings near Pelham Bay.
Along the railtracks sere fairways with plastic bags
during a cold winter. In bare woods of maples, fir,
a lost man curls in his cardboard hut against wind—
ballbreaker cough and incoming rounds everywhere.
He dreams sometimes of a woman who grinned
from a scrapbook picture under broken cartons.
She turns toward him as he shakes and spits,
holding brass hair piled on her head in place
with one hand, kohled eyes blurred, fluttering.
She points to show him redwinged blackbirds
nesting in boxes on poles, or mallards lined up
on water. Their feathers shine in early sunlight.

Reading *New York*

Smells now like rain. Low scud from the west.
I have no thought what it might mean
though I would as soon not get wet but there
it is. So what about Christa Worthington

who got stabbed on Cape Cod by someone?
I think I might know who it was just
from today's news. The press is wild
with stuff like this but comes closer

than the cops have so far to a name.
"I'm not afraid of you. Get out of my house!"
must have been quite loud at the end
and to think our cat too came from Halseys.

Might just not have liked the cut of her jib.
Nothing to be done if that was the case. Tried
to deal with it straight on. Did her best
but came out not her own rosesweet self.

Strange how the tail ends of old lines
seem to fray how, rules that should be taught
are not passed on as the good blood thins out
and finally there's no more time for talk.

Transit

The wild dove keeps pace with him and flies
in straight, regular loops like a telephone line
as if holding some odd faith that his bus
will never waver from its lane, heading out
into New Jersey—toward that place in the sky
where the glow of December sun still moves
above the clouds. To the north and south
the air is dark with great banks of clouds
like high black walls. As taxed brakes squeal
he remembers two doves perched side by side
in a small cage placed on the millstone lid
of an old well, to make a sort of table,
a sculpture almost, murmuring in the garden
of his father's house in France one morning.

This, though, is Secaucus in chill early winter,
where the music has no dying fall, a place
marked from the turnpike by poverty grass
stretched along verges of pools filled, oozing
with the corrosive piss of industry.
In New Brunswick cardboard cutouts
of carolers are spotlit. Anxious wooden
soldiers with redcheeks and bearskin hats
on leave from the *Nutcracker*, honor guards
at Johnson & Johnson—or is it Macy's?—
he cannot tell. The bus glides past.

It is a local now, filled with people not yet undone,
not commuters, their single or conjunctive lives
bound to real place by place where they get on
or get off, who have the wherewithal to buy here
a Greek Gyro, there a Schlitz, or whose keys fit

and power a Buick, not a Mazda or a Ford.
Their next-stop bells call their familiars, signs
that they are home, or near home, their flagdowns
those of the tired, thankful, bitter, cold, exalted,
shattered or relieved. Known and unknown, faces
alive with years of choice, result, acceptance.
He hurries these thoughts along in darkness,
half an hour from that corner where everything
may wait forever, just as he left it, or not.

The dislocation is complete. Deracinated, drifting
through New Jersey in a small box of light,
he mulls streetsigns, stares at banks, plazas,
a chiropractic center. Stallion Pizza in Hidden Lakes.
The answer's silent, somewhere in the ghostly brush
along the roadside—a whisper among dried stalks
of mallow, among moldering stumps in fields.
He seeks in the window's mirror himself—
the withheld approval at midlife he might at five
more happily have had. Karate, Christmas trees,
families, one pub with a penguin's name
next to a Reformed church, something called
a future store. Wang's Kitchen. Such a lark
to seek meaning or patterns where there are none.
Once in Vermont he heard Vaughan's poetry
coming from a burned-out motel near Bennington—
a wheel of fire turned slowly in the air for him.
Now the fear, the search, some shred of certainty
in his head denied him, leaves Grace out in Jersey:
at Kendall Park a drunk with a gimme cap says,
"Thank you, Sire," as he alights beside a mall.

"We are emptying out in the country," he thinks,
"and might as well be lost." Near a cemetery
"grave blankets" are on sale, wreaths and lights.
 He wants to run to his father's burial place
to warm the vestige of that poor, large, angry man,
who counted backwards sequences of numbers,
but was not granted Grace to leave as he wished,
and explain to him that all is forgiven, all restored.

There is a glow still in the west, still hurrying near
above the highway's blue arc lights. To the north
and south, great banks of clouds, pitch black,
spread in the sky like walls, like caves, like wings.

Organ grinder

Cold never got the Italian hurdy-gurdy man when he came
to our street every Friday around lunchtime cranking songs
and occasionally throwing back his head to bellow lyrics
in his heavy raw accent, especially God Bless America
though only the God Bless America part itself, heartfelt,
nothing of mountains or prairies that he'd never seen here.
On the other side of the worn wooden box with two wheels
from where the grinding handle was, rode a yellowed photo
under something like isinglass of three young hunters smiling
in a meadow or a marsh with shotguns, dogs and dead birds
that I used to think around age nine was near the reservoir
about a mile from our house. I reasoned much later
they were probably shooting then near Genoa, Venice
or somewhere in Tuscany before WWI or just after it
and that he had this image always near to remind him
as he sang out for nickels and dimes to us children
of himself with his friends who had perhaps died
long ago. My mother gave me a nickle usually
if I happened to be home instead of in school to tuck
into his cracked cardboard hand. Once in spring
he asked if he could pick dandelions by our driveway.
He took the greens and wrapped them in a blue towel,
grinning and nodding. Good, good, zuppa, he said,
laid his package on the hurdy-gurdy and walked away.

On understanding

Hard lines of the ankle as she places her shoe's heel
just there on a tan carpet, and her voice—a stream
breaking over many stones, folding and refolding
itself—as she talks to no one of an errant earring.
Her language is perhaps Eastern, with English
at crucial junctures: "No, no, don't do that (unknown)"
as the jewel descends inside her dress
like smuggled goods, or an unwanted hand.

As he watches his city rush down and away
while the plane banks up, he thinks his life
was never meant to be what it is, that in voyaging,
remaking, he has for a moment lost connection
with himself, that his own language has grown pidgin
as he, too, gropes among effects for something
suddenly lost, suddenly adrift close by, but threatening
to disappear, untranslated, while he struggles to name it.

Noise

His mouth stretched open, he yells without sound
to deal with the altitude—pressure in his ears—
and memories. Sun bright between fronts
after days of rain, late November, flying south.
The plane belts along two miles above wide
Massachusetts landscape of his *mestizo* childhood.
Taking off, he saw bluey-green copper roofs
near the State House that mark, for now, home.

In a drizzled street on his way to work last month
someone off her meds screamed just this way—
mouth open, no noise, over and over, eyes popped,
like a person blown out a hatch into dark voids,
beyond maybe Pluto—like hollering to the catcher
from centerfield, knowing you won't be heard in time.

The small plane's engines whelm even a pilot's voice,
carrying some tenor tidbit about "our current position."
Or perhaps it's blocked ears. (What is not heard and seen
cannot be known, can only be guessed, fictioned,
like a life unlived—all episodes imaginary, dreamed,
except those few which still make people cry silently
in their chairs at home, rocking gently forward, back,
forward, clutching a handkerchief, grinding teeth,
their mouths sometimes opening to form names
not spoken in the right way, or called out in time.)

Far down, etched by late morning sun, a V of geese
bears southwest across vast dumps and piggeries
sprawled outward from New York: "Those are birds
that were my thoughts. . . ." He thinks, therefore

they fly, could not cry out each to each to mark a turn
without his words and recollections to inform them.

In this silent enterprise, putting things down
on paper two miles above a golf course, tank farm,
cemetery, factory, tract house or black pond,
lies resolution, answer to void and grave misery,
reconstruction of the formless or destroyed. Why
he flies is not as sure as why, while a younger man
across the aisle computes the values of collateral,
he writes on a yellow, wide-lined paper on his lap.

Marine Landscape

Here on the train as you might remember
there are glimpses of marsh or the Sound.
One wide bay carries a small boat, anchored,
with two figures against the shining water
perhaps trying their luck among the mackerel—
who can know from this distance or at this speed?

With brimmed hats and poles sticking up,
they are quite like another two, softly afloat
in the little painting beside our bed at home
that we bought in New Hampshire one summer.
Not knowing subject, artist, provenance
made it no less wonderful a discovery.

And now, in this changeable time,
what shall we do? Anchor here or row
further, to another spot? Do not answer.
Remember that I am on a train.

Consecutive pages

There again, jade-green harbor in late afternoon,
big plane's shadow gliding down over water, or
movements reflected in a TV screen, unconnected,
blurry regions between observed and imagined,
where "insights" reign and careful words mean
other things to another—flying, for instance, love,
being alone—always dim motions where pebbles,
waves, grasses merge beyond this runway coming in
beside stone jetties in winter, or where ghosts of man,
cat, table, sofa glimmer over a test pattern at dawn.
Remembering that "night is the body of someone else,"
he gets up, goes down to get his paper at the door.

Newspaper Days

From my office window I look up and out
into the bluest of blue skies—fading contrail
pointing southwest possibly New York too high
to be a shuttle as close as this to Logan—no
it must have come across the Atlantic today
from Paris, London, maybe Warsaw where also
it was yesterday the birthday of Czeslaw Milosz
whose name is mispronounced by many who
should know better than to hazard a try without
benefit of Polish or better still Lithuanian.
These idylls flitterings of a dull aging boredom
on a perfect summer day. Now there are clouds
little puffs and another contrail even higher
and for relief click on nytimes to find another
story of the right length to get into but not too.
Finding thoughts to catch as consciousness
moves inward outward. When I was young
my mother said Don't be Tiresome in her best
clipped British tones from Adelaide while she
struggled even then to make sense of her day
by turning to yet another task for which she
had had no preparation on Strangways Terrace
overlooking the city with Mount Lofty behind.
To avoid being either Tiresome or her other one
Tedious, my little boy went fossicking inside
his head using pieces of outside to make stories
or arrange events of the right length to get into—
not too far taking no more than a few minutes
or about an average newspaper column's read.

Happenings in 1992

> "That's how it is, Mister, you know?
>   Everything is made out of mess."
> *NY cabdriver*

Los Angeles

It is a jacaranda after all—the blue purple
not a dream. Yet the image is almost fiction:
startling blast of color like a loud shirt
in the scrub, among the live oaks, palms
and eucalyptus along an airport access road.
When leaves replace blooms, unreality wanes,
trees become trees again, not startling blasts
of color in the smoke along an airport road.

Dreams

I fear a standing figure, its face in darkness.
The house smells of death. I'm grinding my teeth
in sleep these days, I run out of air, cry unheard
about nothing.

The men change into coveralls
in a shed, balls showing on a pier in Cherbourg.
It is early morning and they are laughing.
My mother says, "Hurry up. Don't stare."

San Francisco

Looking down from the 23rd floor off Market,
wedged behind a low table, I am an angel
above it all, like the heavenly host in hymns.

95

There is room service, and Cosby interlaced on TV
with helicopters I can see and hear outside, and LA
on fire and dying truckers. Next door, far below,
under glass, Japanese swim laps in a hotel pool.
This is the strangest ever. Children in the street
change their sneakers for $90 Nikes, scattered
red paper out of boxes boosted from The Gap,
blowing up the street as motorcycle cops close in.

Boston Common

South Church's safe bells play electric hymns.
"How you doin', big guy? Got a quarter for me?
Help me out?" Michael flown to Earth again
on his bench near the State House in morning.
He wears a pale blue wool cap and he sweats.
"Did I tell you my dream when I had to go home?
Someone knocked. I went downstairs.
Two guys at the door, drug guys. Want to come in,
big one says. I say no, but they was coming.
So I hit him. He fell. I kicked him good.
But the other one was by me, up the stairs,
looking for my mother. That's it. Have a good day."

Living backwards

Tourists take pictures of our house in the rain.
Our cats scurry around, radiators knock,
and that Christmas tree's still in the window.
Retrograde, unpinned, I am having dreams
that do not finish or make sense, aware
of a car rolling back downhill somewhere
long ago, without lights or brakes.
Maybe it was in a film, or someone's story.

Once there was a party with many people
in a big house. Now there is a telephone ringing,
noisy pipes, and other families calling out
across a street, where lights in their apartment
make it possible for me to see my way
to the bathroom in darkness like those lit
for the same reason when I cried in bed
because I saw Germans coming, then slept.

The dark rhododendrons where I played
are here now. I am in them, hiding but waving.
There is a garden out over which I soared
on a plank knotted by my father at the ends
of two ropes hung from a pinetree branch
near our chicken coop before he went to war.

This is a tidy place, and Lord knows, my dear,
we've made it something grand from not much.
But I'm getting old, and when you're not here,
I hold on all night to keep from slipping back.
When the sun comes up, I am sinfully happy.

Spring on Beacon Hill

Having no proper gift for her, don't be silent,
or become a gray stone cloud. Study instead
the sound of falling water outside your window,
beneath traffic noise and continuous whining
of some eternal burglar alarm. It is spillover
from that pitched slate roof, falling four floors
into a rolling surf of lilac bushes, grass, bricks.
No sound when rain began, but at full torrent,
its roar is louder than wind. Think this a time
of sudden noises and vistas, which you discover
not in aches, pains, complaints, fear of loss,
but in catching up with an odor of daffodils
along the sidewalk, or from a woman you love—
a zone in moist air that you enter like walking
through a curtain, then note meticulously after rain
that the first white flowering twigs on branches
along your street are those closest to the lights.

Short takes in Vermont

    S.

The kingfisher flew upstream,
slicing, dipping, its stern head
and white slash all he really saw.

My memory's jest shot to hell
he said, propped on one elbow
in the grass, affecting hayseed talk.

Moving his head sideways, he watched
a large, distant cloud, like an animal,
silently investigate her hair, her shoulder.

The way the leaves look like fingers—
the way those leaves look today you'd think
I don't know what—pianos, lovers.

Wind's from the northwest, she said,
and weather's from the southwest. In August
you just can't tell how long until it clears.

I'M THE ONLY HELL MY MOTHER
EVER RAISED on a pickup's front bumper—
beard, Coors gimme cap, dark shades.

I'm not up to pisspot entanglements
in this heat—don't have energy enough
to eat, let alone screw around.

She showed up one night in a chamois chemise
with nothing underneath. When this gets
tiresome, I can use it to polish the car.

Gracious what a struggle, she said,
her laugh curling around him.
You're the biggest man I ever knew.

At noon he molests yellow flowers,
walking close to where they sun,
casually whispering obscenities.

Those tears are just to keep him
in line, said the neighbor's wife.
She's got his balls in a mangle.

One bird outside his window
sings lonely lonely honey,
another betrayed betrayed.

Against the wall in a wooden niche
stands Saint Francis, apologetically
wringing his hands over this natural world.

Making the Paper House, Rockport, Mass.

"Work covered a period of twenty years"

How many times did he turn to his wife
and ask her to hold the rolled *Transcript*
tight while he applied shellac? Did they
have a system? Did a truck door open outside
at six, spilling the day's unpurchased copies
of Boston's papers out in a stream as if
in a cartoon of death's evacuation?

Where is the joy in such constancy?
He longs for a phone call, rolling sheets
nervously in his hands like a young boy
on the edge of a sofa without protection,
waiting for his girlfriend in her parents' parlor
mouth shut, with the lights on and shades up.

She dips newsprint in a pan without attention,
doing what must be done on the floor
between them, hoping for an end to this tedium,
this blunted desire, continuous interruption.

She is tired. He is tired. Both have access
to language beyond their capacities. A fire
now surely couldn't burn much of anything
that they might say was their very own.

At the ballpark

Sweetheart, the long middle of this game
floats like a blooper lost in the sun
or fuzz in my warm cup of draft, he thinks.
He dreams there is a homerun hit somewhere
and wills the ball up, come on, get out,
get over everything into the carlot,
behind green walls, spreading your star
on some big Toronado's windshield, baby.
He wakes, drive's snared on one hop—
it happens that fast—in centerfield.

Arrival in Pittsburgh

Upstream from New Kensington, north of Moon Run,
towns and farms hold down each corner or center
of the patterned land, each with its own spring,
its own grays, browns, yellows, becoming green.
On some hills, tossed suddenly up from the dark,
ribbed ground which no leaves hide, shell-bursts
of white blossoms in a low sun's slant topography
mark the movement of whole forests toward light.

In this 4:30 Friday pale afternoon haze
do barges really move past those smooth banks
seen from 25,000 feet above the Allegheny?
So it would seem from the furrowed trail
of lime-colored wash in a slow S back
all the way around a bend, slowly merging
a mile downstream with the other greens.
Or perhaps they never really move at all.

In the last moments as glide slips past thrust
and into that final few hundred feet of gravity,
Lord, let me be safe and sound this thousandth time.
This is, indeed, it. The bouncing always makes me
a believer for a moment. Then, as often in the brush
off runways, there are comforting mounds of detritus—
tires and rust, old signs, bits of cable, some record
of people working here beside the hard cement.

Buffalo Shuffle

2 girls probably
thought narc
in waterbed store
Buffalo rain

said restaurant
next door
pure shit

bolted garbage
came back
believer

cold girls bored
betrayal
lonely motel
drank all TV

Santa Monica evening

He is careful sliding his windows open
and the moth spirals out—its stuttering wings
now only a minor distraction, a memory like glass,
without answers. And there are none from the ocean,
sun evaporating behind that dark coastal slope,
while pale blue fog hovers like a worried saint
just off the beach, stretching to the horizon's line,
the whole void now of boats, no birds, no waves.

Middleaged men on the beach

They think it's such a distance up the dunes from here.
They ponder all the delectable calves, thighs, breasts,
thinking of sex, dreaming of youth, of hard-ons,
of painless entries or exits, mindless ejaculations,
and of a generosity that might suddenly give
them so much more of this, more of that.

Asopo

The dying Wolf Moon's *plateyes* mess with me,
raising black arms from holes no bigger
than a man's touched forefinger and thumb
to grapple me in sleep and roll my bed.
O Lord, we are sore afraid of silence here.
The island hums with Bosomworth's betrayed,
angry dreams of small empire—a dark marriage
burned off by Oglethorpe's whiskey and a patience
superior to theirs because more civil.

Then Morel's straight-out gallops to South End—
thoroughbreds smashed into trees in the moonlight's
grey moss, bones crumbling behind palms, rice crops
a failure, catch of breath after quiet footsteps.
Trees with manacles—the walking ghost matched strides
with them as the boys returned from dancing—him *slabey*
doing his last juke then, heels beating wateroak bark
one two three one two three   one.

In the center of the midden the great snake sleeps,
tail wrapped round the knot of the world,
oyster shells his house—old offerings and supplications.
In certain lights, odd times of day, winds risen suddenly,
men alone moved warily along green tunnels of eyes,
through shudders of palms, their skin moistening
in the creases of bellies or hollows of necks—
earth, water, sky the enemies because unmoved.
Quarrying graveyards, carving up marshes, hunting
to kill not eat, shoveling, filling in, burying,
a community of solitaries revenged itself,
protected by motion and sheer quantity—

its broken china, glazed ware, bottles, buttons, hinges
not so much disdain as desperation.
(If all around me is my own detritus, my own
free-fire zone, no *plateyes*, bones, shell piles,
winds, waves or manacles will capture me.
I cross the threshold thus, I cross myself thus,
I turn and look, throw down my rusted iron thus.)

Our rituals have no deities at center.
Offal in a cul-de-sac magics no sudden openings.
We have worked out our terror on this landscape,
reshaping, crushing what we could not match with force.
Our plastic shards within palmetto clumps outlast
coon's oysters, whelk, flint, riverstones
because they must. One quick white flash—
or brushfire in May—would not return
but add them to the dust. Inside stockades
high-booted Oglethorpes pen flesh and blood away,
those few sweet sighs in shadow which we fled,
sweating, instead of opening with desire.

Six wheeling copters craze the marsh with sound.

Notes to "Asopo": Asopo is the Native American name for Ossabaw Island, one of the Georgia Sea Islands, located just south of Savannah. The area was subdued and settled by Colonel James Oglethorpe in the 1730s. *Plateyes* are malicious spirits. The word is Gullah, a dialect still spoken by some of the African American inhabitants of these islands, descendents of West African slaves (hence *slabey*). The Reverend Thomas Bosomworth, originally with the British Army, attached to Oglethorpe, married a half-breed woman named Maria Musgrove. The two of them laid claim to the island, citing her Native American ancestry, and were ultimately put down by the English and deprived of their "nation." Ossabaw was planted with long staple cotton and indigo, and, for a brief period, with rice. It was farmed by the Morel family, in one part or another, for about 150 years. Its roads are paved with crushed oyster shells taken from a large shell midden, one of several on the island, dating from Native American occupations. Coon's oysters are the shells left by raccoons near the brackish pools where they often wash their food. During the Viet Nam War, Ossabaw was used as a training flight area for helicopter gunships stationed near Savannah. The poem was begun in January 1972, when I was a guest at the Ossabaw Island Project—then a haven for artists and writers under the auspices of Eleanor Torrey West.

Karachi 1953

I swam beside but not in the Indus. It really
isn't safe my aunt said so I stuck to the club pool
even when there was a race from a barge to the dock
that I might have won. Later a sunroofed taxi took
me from the walled suburban villa to a cinema where
something with Donald O'Connor was playing. A camel
drooled on me through the open hatch as we were stopped
in traffic. Inside I sat in a darkened box with curtains
and was stared at until the lights went out. One bright
morning I lay on my bed looking out the window
as a BOAC Comet took off maybe five miles away
shooting suddenly almost straight up which was why
so many of them crashed it turned out later. On a sofa
in the living room I listened to Grieg's A minor piano
concerto on 78. It was the first piece of "classical" music
that wasn't a theme for the Green Hornet or Lone Ranger.
I can remember having to change disks again and again.
Someone young with a carload of children of various ages
took me to the beach on Sunday. They made shandygaffs
of lemon soda and beer and gave me a glass which was First
Alcohol Ever. Chipper and foolhardy at 13 I tormented
a moray eel from rocks above a pool using a curtain rod
that it struck many times. It let go when I pulled the rod out.
My uncle on the day before we left hired a snakecharmer
who squatted on the walk in front of our house and played
an instrument like a clarinet while a cobra really did come
out of a basket pushing the lid up with his puffed mantle
and falling down on the grass seeming to get away
so my cousins screamed but the charmer grabbed
it and pulled it back holding its head away from his face
putting it into the basket again. In the distance huge ghats

with vultures circling which is where you'd end if you were
a Parsee and let that snake bite you said my uncle. While
I packed the houseboy brought me a round straw cap
and orange silk to make a turban and showed me how.
This was Pakistan six years after its terrible beginning.
We were friends. I promised to write him from America.

Ghat—An Aide-Memoire

Oblivion's swift: here a truck marked
"Goods Carrier" there a crushed car
in bushes by the road. Now people
squatting in a village field with crows.
Later carts loaded with everything
owners on top. Goats buffalo birds
children tugging. Man with a cow
and stick (all cows go home at night).
Hinayana, Mahayana. One billion
manifestations of Krishna in this
subsistent world we rush through.
Small fish flicker out of the water
jumping for life. Dolphins cruise past.

Good Friday in Kyoto

I was taught as a kid to hate
Japs and their country—invaders
murdering people with bombs, swords,
starvation, beating my uncle in a camp
so that he shrank two inches. So I did.

Now I am among them. They are friendly—
maybe because of the atom bomb, maybe
just that I don't read them right. It's
so hard to forget floating bodies in *Life*,
flames and machine guns, my Australian
mother afraid of invasion, Brelis killing
them, some with his bare hands. *Arrigato*.

Good Friday brings Jesus to Kyoto. His
white stone outstretched familiar hands
palms up beseeching outside a small R.C.
chapel on a narrow street. Our martial arts
sensei invokes Him as another valid origin
of strength and cosmic force-giver.
The Jewish kid from Amherst who translates
for this strongman misses a beat on that,
and why not? It's Passover. In 60 years
hatred has gone all haywire. Skipping
through town that August evening banging
with a spoon on a saucepan beside Grandpop
to celebrate Surrender becomes curious dread
preparing to visit Hiroshima. Now gone
from ignoring Arabs to fearing them, and
one's own country once so brave careening

around the world killing thousands who want
to live, believing its own bloody propaganda
about "God," "Freedom" and "Democracy."

Here in Kyoto it takes bean curd wrapped
in a leaf and green tea to bring perspective
to this time and even that . . . even that.
Not miso soup, not rice, not pickled radish
can begin to reconcile this ghastliness. A Zen
garden of sand and stones no good, either.
When I visited, it was drowned in hundreds
of chattering schoolchildren—my old hate
hidden in irritation at those babbling kids.

Bullet train

The face of our lunch-cart man on the *shinkansen*
to Tokyo reveals a state of enlightenment
few achieve as he turns and bows at car's door
while out the window Mount Fuji speeds past.

Flat out in France

Here's how it ran between Brussels and Paris
one early June morning on a fast motorcycle—
an Ariel 650 Huntsmaster made in 1954—
big, cruddy maroon thing, English license,
like a pennant on the front fender, ROE 19,
which I thought one late drunk night
might signify "Roll Over, Europe,"
being then 19 myself, and hungry—
with Lenny Bloom of Sedgwick Avenue,
Bronx NY, riding pillion, holding tight
around my chest, shy, uncomfortable.

Pulled into a BP station just opening
and saw there, while the tank filled up,
this sight—new Jag 3.4 litre, grey, Belgian plates
(red on white), absolutely smashed, a rollover,
towed in by a greasy kid in an old truck,
and saw bloodstains all over , especially noted
bullseyed glass, crushed wheel, how the finish
on the leather seats kept blood from soaking in.

We ate buns, jam, coffee, then pushed on out,
straddled our machine, with Lenny behind, clutching,
mumbling about danger on wet early morning roads.
Kicked down hard to start and in the roar
dreamed my parents dead, wept, moaned,
shook and drove.

He remembers brightness

A large clear sunlit space again—
the square panes, the interior defined
by looking through it from outside—
the greenhouse then one possibility,
existing in a child's memory,
and now, in this burst of light,
an unentered joy to be hungered after.

Here another—Paris or Lyons perhaps,
fooling around a courtyard tank one grey summer—
the clean panes behind him, not central,
war wreckage still uncleared behind walls—
the boy's hand pinched suddenly:
a crayfish held by an aging Frenchman
who lied, laughed, told him not to be afraid.
He angered his parents perhaps, crying.
His fingernail turned blue but did not drop or peel.

And this last now, some later place—
important only because of what grows inside him—
smell of grapefruit blossoms,
a stuffed crow in a bamboo cage, air
not clean, not clear, interior defined
improperly, and only in a certain light,
by looking through to the outside, toward the sea.
Winter, late morning, dark windows.

Hunting on the lagoon

(after a painting by Carpaccio)

O bella vista, loaded with prowling nobility.
What's more, they're poled about by Moors.
Look closely—the artist playing perspectives
while whole new worlds were being found.
No arrows are in flight, no cormorants struggle.
Some birds even seem to ride their killers' boats.
But two at least have had it—their heads trail
in green water. And one, swimming, pulls her belly up
as if she sensed a capped shaft's coming.
Beyond her, on a weir, another airs his wings
with no regard for slaughter. Which are decoys?
And why Mary's lily in the foreground?
"The most beautiful thing I ever saw" inside a window?
or a false view of both worlds, as if the Betrayer,
to breach our faith and shape all possibilities,
offered us the beast with both backs, mounted
in a single frame, exposing in this moment
all unlikelihoods within his deceptive tale?
Still two heads loll, the Moors pole still,
and other birds, with warm, full eyes,
slip here and there, untainted in the waves.

Looking up

Maybe it's a camel or weasel or whale, whatever.
Never lose sight though, my dear, that it is a cloud
up there and not something fancied. From where I sit,
those blobs of steam above are just that—blobs of steam—
whether or not watchers are honest, or the sun shining,
though it's nicest when they're bright with hard edges,
and moving slowly off to the northeast, toward the sea.
Going nowhere on a Friday afternoon, I've got wild songs
in my head and fierce shouts, watching a blue, blue sky.

Under the moon

Why should it be that in their country
when someone dies they say he is
"standing under the moon"? If you
are looking for shelter in a sudden rain
and find it on someone's veranda,
you might hear an exchange like this:
"Where is she these days?"
"Standing under the moon, I'm afraid."
And there are other odd phrases
that make you feel like a stranger
even to yourself. If a person falls
in love, the others say he or she
"has become a tree." There are ways
even to differentiate qualities of intensity
in a relationship, as you might catalogue
a forest, thus, "She is becoming an aspen,"
or, "He has become a hickory this spring."
On occasion I find that I cannot hold myself
together, and my own identity runs off
into this other language, which is a state
well known to them. They call it "going
into a tube," and as they say this phrase,
they often dance, and even find their fathers.

Dream

By Berestoewe's silent sea, shimmering black gray
under oily clouds, with smooth metallic cliffs,
which might be steel machines coated in ice, as far off
as one's mind can reach in sleep, and almost
entirely circling a yellowish horizon,
he stands and sketches at a large board on trestles—
the paper filled with images of rage and grief—
then he raises his face to shout a song in chords
"as if from a profound distance beneath water,"
were there anything at all to be heard by Berestoewe's sea,
named, as you might have guessed, for the explorer, though
he never sailed here, and charted it only by reports
from hunters, sealers, scramblers after whales, ivory,
a hidden passage to slaves, gold, spices—more grandeur
than we here now can ever again at will imagine.

The View

   G.

When I was in Vermont, cruising on a dirt track high up
in the spinal Green Mountains from which the forest hangs,
I slowed down to see a view and noticed instead the flowers
on the verge—blue chickory and Queen Anne's lace waving
in a moment's breeze—that had floated unseen until I looked.
Something about them reminded me of something else, far off
on some page or other of a magazine, or perhaps the *Times*
in its current half-page technicolor bursts of off-news,
like the "Science Times" on Tuesdays, which I always save
because Tuesday becomes Wednesday and on Wednesdays
I have been traveling to New York on Amtrak and need
attention-fodder. I saw the Queen Anne's lace clusters
were pointed every whichway, the sun not yet having risen
far enough to reach out and grip them, turning all to look,
and that in this mode they seemed to be a hundred thousand
galaxies receding silently whirling toward the far view
I thought I was going to look at when I slowed down,
each in its own plane, on its own course toward that nothing.

GROWTH

Postcard

We rest a lot,
then all night I go
torching in the swamp.
Swinging my big nets
in the smoke, I take
shiners, eel, redfish,
frogs, shrimp, whatever
else may flutter up,
into my baskets.
Those day did not do in
swim wildly up into
this other sunlight.

Growing again

Began last night at fifty feet an hour—
all carefully measured and surveyed today,
a frightened boy came with his theodolite.

I staggered and unfurled the first eight feet.
My dog ran from me with curious groans,
peed on a nearby stone, went home.

Today he lifted leg again (televised)
on my heel. My big problem is to void
without statewide catastrophe.

My well-wishers are here.
(Their half-mile neighbor!)
They have their fears.

Half awake half dead

My heart is hooved, stubbornly
clopping in this fouled stall bed.
My wife, sensible, needing her sleep,
gets up and goes to another room, across
a wide river of dreamed kindness offering
her own best loved comfort. "Try some heat,"
she says as she shuts the door.

It isn't flu, or wine I drank, or lack of exercise,
or pain, or medicine I take more from habit
than need. I'm not chilled. I want to go
shake her in her bed and shout,
"It's memory's wild horse, Fear.
And there's no cure."

In bed

You could come to realize this:
what you say is interesting
because you are interesting
because your thinking makes
it all right at the end.
That you can astonishes
that this can be done
that they can in fact
sit still inside your
head without coughing
talking wishing to go.
This may be a simple revelation
not unlike the quick cold dream
that if you open your eyes here
in the darkness or move a muscle
something beside you will strike.

The true sense of the real is change

said the sculptor.
A small red "inDian" is
yesterday's picture, its
provenance my daughter's seventh year
(her mind gone chasing deer then, truly).
Now there is now to heal.

Matter of saying is my matter—
the oddness all untied,
untruths dealt out,
the spell sung   pain undone.

The moon changes.
Blood goes to be remade. There is
the inDian's smile to call
"the real"

Paint

That, Madam, is paint, he said to a NY lady
who wondered about a portion of some work
unremembered otherwise hung in the Daniel
Gallery as recorded by Williams in his memoir—
a moment he suggests as beginning modernism—
not imitating but being the natural world.

No way to observe similar intention in print,
As for all those other media, there is
always and forever Time. It is certainly
an important aspect of my work, a woman
with Brillo hair from Colombia observed
when pressed about her coupling wooden tables.

How then to give to writing some semblance
of mystery, as in that's paint, not a known shape,
not even a timed or timeless Latin table or two?
What shibboleth might we employ that would
distinguish our labor, allow it to stand clear,
complete in itself, and not as figure for another?

Perhaps a stone poem—an Acheulean scraper
carefully flaked in brown flint—so people
treat it as an object with unknown meaning,
or no now meaning, no usefulness, beautiful
as a random spot on that butterfly's wing,
some late afternoon splash of color on a wall.

5 × 8 card

Check Yeats about decrepitude/wisdom again.
Pound's "broken bundle of mirrors" to mind.
Further from rhetoric: whacked-out fragments
"where one needs one's brains all the time."
Remember? Are you there now? Puzzled
by the time it takes (is *form*—Gus Solomons, Jr.)
and trying to snap pictures, too: make odd things
still always.
Perhaps wrong action. Read thinkers.
Not instant-stopper *inside* (you); not high energy,
deep need for calm. Read self: more radarscreen
than halfback in Finley's metaphors. But then
you didn't know him. Do I know you? You me?
Slow down. Watch out. Think *where*, not *how*/*when*.
Gently. It's all we get—one start, one road.

Archery

In aiming, aiming's all.
It should command each cell's attention—
this straining toward finding
one pure tunnel in the air
requires a center. Don't move, keep
muscles tensed, low to the ground,
hard and ready. Don't be distracted.
Hunker down and hold your passion
as a seed pod holds seed until
the moment's right. You will
not feel the letting go.

Navigator

He's still uncertain how he does it—
keeps everything afloat on this ocean—
or even if he should bother after all.

This isn't fun anymore, he thinks,
but recites the unnameable's
I can't go on I'll go on. Pride

won't let him stop here and drop
anchor far short of the shoreline.
It is a perplex of significance:

this jumbled sea of loops and snarls
all pulling and rubbing like Kon-Tiki
on its slow conjectural way west

across the Pacific disintegrating
gently among nighttime swells,
luminescence, whispering voices.

Swallowtails

Can that be right? Can the score be summed
in such a way? He sat and read, he sang—
there was no music. Was there text?

He has cocoons in his kitchen.
Playing with the jars they're spun in
does them harm—they slip and dry.

This morning two dark cases made it through,
evicting tenants whose small terrific glory
showed him midnight sunsets during breakfast.

He hung them on the parsley, staring,
as they waved their wings to fill them,
possessed, like them, with waiting.

A lesson in their sudden flight—
slim process bears if left alone.
That said, he goes inside to spin and change.

Geoffrey Movius lives in Cambridge and Gloucester, Massachusetts. In an earlier life, he was author of *The Early Prose of William Carlos Williams* (Garland Press), scholarly articles on Williams and Ezra Pound, and published interviews with Jerzy Kosinski and Susan Sontag. He then worked for 30 years as a development officer for Harvard University in New York, Boston, Los Angeles and San Francisco. His poetry has appeared in little magazines since the 1960s.